PROFILES

Bob Geldof
Chris May

Illustrated by
Brian Denington
and
Diana Bowles

Hamish Hamilton
London

Titles in the Profiles *series*

Ian Botham	0-241-12293-7	Martin Luther King	0-241-10931-0
Edith Cavell	0-241-11479-9	Nelson Mandela	0-241-11913-8
Marie Curie	0-241-11741-0	Bob Marley	0-241-11476-4
Roald Dahl	0-241-11043-2	The Queen Mother	0-241-11030-0
Thomas Edison	0-241-10713-X	Florence Nightingale	0-241-11477-2
Margot Fonteyn	0-241-12506-5	Emmeline Pankhurst	0-241-11478-0
Anne Frank	0-241-11294-X	Anna Pavlova	0-241-10481-5
Elizabeth Fry	0-241-12084-5	Prince Philip	0-241-11167-6
Gandhi	0-241-11166-8	Beatrix Potter	0-241-12051-9
Indira Gandhi	0-241-11772-0	Viv Richards	0-241-12046-2
Bob Geldof	0-241-12295-3	Barry Sheene	0-241-10851-9
Amy Johnson	0-241-12317-8	Mother Teresa	0-241-10933-7
Helen Keller	0-241-11295-8	Queen Victoria	0-241-10480-7
John F. Kennedy	0-241-12288-0	The Princess of Wales	0-241-11740-2
John Lennon	0-241-11561-2		

The author and publisher would like to thank
Bob Geldof and Marsha Hunt
for their help and cooperation.

HAMISH HAMILTON CHILDREN'S BOOKS

Published by the Penguin Group
27 Wrights Lane, London W8 5TZ, England
Viking Penguin Inc., 40 West 23rd Street, New York, New York 10010, U.S.A.
Penguin Books Australia Ltd, Ringwood, Victoria, Australia
Penguin Books Canada Ltd, 2801 John Street, Markham, Ontario, Canada L3R 1B4
Penguin Books (N.Z.) Ltd, 182–190 Wairau Road, Auckland 10, New Zealand

Penguin Books Ltd, Registered Offices: Harmondsworth, Middlesex, England

First published in Great Britain 1988 by
Hamish Hamilton Children's Books

Text copyright © 1988 by Chris May
Illustrations copyright © 1988 by Brian Denington and Diana Bowles

All rights reserved. Without limiting the rights under copyright reserved above, no part of this publication may be reproduced, stored in or introduced into a retrieval system or transmitted, in any form or by any means (electronic, mechanical, photocopying, recording or otherwise), without the prior written permission of both the copyright owner and the above publisher of this book.

British Library Cataloguing in Publication Data
May, Chris
Bob Geldof. — (Profiles).
1. Geldof, Bob   2. Rock musicians —
Ireland — Biography — Juvenile literature
I. Title   II. Series
784.5′4′00924   ML420.G328
ISBN 0-241-12295-3

Typeset by Pioneer

Printed in Great Britain at the
University Press, Cambridge

For Saffron and Catherine

Contents

1	'THE GREATEST DAY OF MY LIFE'	11
2	DARK DAYS	14
3	A CARING REBEL	18
4	A TIME OF CHANGE	21
5	THE BOOMTOWN RATS	25
6	'LOOKIN' AFTER NUMBER ONE'	29
7	A NEW GENERATION	33
8	'DO THEY KNOW IT'S CHRISTMAS?'	37
9	LIVE AID	44
10	'THIS IS THE WORLD CALLING'	50
	Important events in the life of Bob Geldof	57
	Summary of Band Aid's Aims	59

Bob Geldof

1 'The greatest day of my life'

The thirteenth of July 1985 was a hot, sunny day in Britain. It was the sort of day when most people would have been lying about in their gardens or relaxing in the park. But today there were few people about in the streets. Despite the beautiful weather, everybody seemed to be indoors watching television. There was something else unusual too — the same sounds were drifting out of open living room windows. Almost every household was tuned into a pop concert being staged simultaneously at London's Wembley Stadium and at another stadium in Philadelphia, U.S.A.

Streets were also deserted in many countries all over the world. Whatever the weather was like, the majority of people were indoors watching the pop concert.

The concert was Live Aid: the biggest and most important rock show ever held. It was the biggest because of the huge global television audience, but its importance was much more significant. The concert was not being held to make money for pop stars and their record companies, but to raise money to buy food and shelter for 22 million people in Africa who were starving to death in the worst famine ever known.

Live Aid was the biggest rock show in another way

too. Appearing on stage in London and Philadelphia was the most spectacular collection of pop stars ever to sing in one concert. The list was long, including such famous names as Paul McCartney, Elton John, Mick Jagger, Phil Collins, Duran Duran, Paul Young, the Beach Boys, the Style Council, Simple Minds and David Bowie. Mick Jagger and David Bowie made a special video to be premièred at the event. Phil Collins appeared at Wembley and then flew in Concorde to Philadelphia to perform there that evening. None of these people were being paid to appear at Live Aid; every penny that was raised was going to be spent on famine relief in Africa.

Among the other stars taking part at Wembley were the Boomtown Rats, led by their singer, Bob Geldof. No longer a major force in the pop charts, the Rats were there because the entire Live Aid event — and the Band Aid record which had preceded it — had been Bob's idea. It was he who had first been determined to mount this massive exercise in famine relief and he who had persuaded other people, inside and outside the music business, to join in. Without Bob none of it would have happened.

It had taken him nine long, hard months to organise Live Aid. During the concert, in front of 80,000 people at Wembley Stadium and on television screens all over the world, Bob stopped the Rats in the middle of their song 'I Don't Like Mondays'. He raised his fist above his head and silence fell over the crowd. After what seemed like a very long time, Bob said, 'I think this must be the greatest day of my life.'

For many years, Bob had been searching for a purpose. Up until recently, he felt his only real achievement was being part of the Boomtown Rats — and even the success of the Rats had been shortlived. But on that hot summer day in 1985, in front of millions of people across the world, Bob was finally able to look inside himself and feel good about what he saw.

2 Dark Days

Robert Frederick Zenon Geldof was born on 5 October 1952. He lived with his mother and father, and elder sisters Lynn and Cleo, in a small house in Blackrock Park, Dublin, the capital city of Eire.

Bob remembers his early childhood as a happy and contented time. His father worked as a travelling salesman, driving around Eire selling crockery and glassware. He only came home at weekends, but despite this, the family was close and loving. Although Bob's father did not earn a lot of money, Bob's parents always made sure that their children had everything they needed. However, the Geldofs could not afford a television and when Bob wanted to watch children's programmes he had to go down the road to a friend's house. Bob read a lot and his favourite books were adventure stories, like *Swiss Family Robinson* and *Ivanhoe*.

The Geldofs were Catholics and when he was eight years old Bob made his First Holy Communion, a very important event in the life of a Catholic. It was a tradition, after the ceremony, for friends and relations to give small gifts of money to a new communicant. Bob spent all that he was given on a plastic guitar!

Bob with his father and sisters, Cleo and Lynn

But these happy years were not to last. A series of sad events were to affect Bob very badly. First, one of his friends died of leukaemia (a disease of the blood), and shortly afterwards Bob's family moved to a new house in another part of Dublin. He remembers the house as a dark and forbidding place. Not long after the family had moved home, Bob's mother died suddenly from a brain haemorrhage. He was especially close to his mother, so the shock of her death was particularly strong for him. Perhaps Bob would have found it easier to cope with his sorrow if he had still been surrounded by all his old friends at Blackrock Park. He had to grieve, however, in a new neighbourhood and a house he did not feel comfortable in.

Bob's father continued working as a travelling salesman, so Bob's eighteen-year-old sister Cleo was put in charge of the house. Bob and Lynn would go to school while Cleo cleaned and mended their clothes, cooked their meals and generally looked after things at home.

Shortly after Bob's mother had died, tragedy almost struck again. Cleo was told by doctors that she was suffering from leukaemia and had only a few months to live. Although Bob was not told about this at the time, he sensed that something was very wrong and this made him even more unhappy. Desperate to find a cure, Cleo made a pilgrimage to Lourdes, in France. Many Catholics believe that Lourdes was once visited by the Virgin Mary and for centuries sick people have gone there in the hope of a miracle cure. Miracle or not, when Cleo returned to Dublin, she no longer had

Blackrock College — the school Bob attended

leukaemia. She is still alive and well today.

During this difficult time, Bob had become sulky and withdrawn, and he started to get into trouble at school. No longer interested in his lessons, he frequently missed classes, preferring to wander around the Dublin streets. When he did attend school he was disobedient and lazy. His school was extremely strict, and Bob was often beaten because of his behaviour. His father also punished him for his lack of effort at school. Bob felt the injustice of this treatment and rebelled even more.

3 A Caring Rebel

By the time he was fourteen years old, Bob seemed to be a very different person to the cheerful, well-behaved boy he had once been. His family and teachers thought him rude and lazy, only interested in pop records and hanging around in coffee bars.

Deep down Bob was, of course, the same person. But the death of his mother, combined with his increasing dislike of school, was making him more and more unhappy. Bob expressed this unhappiness by rebelling against adults. If they wanted him to work hard in lessons, then he would show them how difficult he could be. If they wanted him to look neat and tidy, then he would look as sloppy and dishevelled as possible.

At this time, 1966, the two most popular groups in Britain and Eire were the Beatles and the Rolling Stones. People of all ages liked the Beatles, while the Stones appealed mainly to teenagers. The Beatles had long hair, but they wore suits and their songs had pretty melodies. The Stones, on the other hand, had a rebellious image. This appealed to Bob and he became a keen fan of the Stones' music, as well as their behaviour.

He was determined to be a rebel, which meant being

Bob spent a lot of spare time in the local record shop

against everything. Later, he would realise that he could rebel and yet be *for* certain things; that he could try to change the world for the better rather than simply to give up and kick against it.

Gradually, Bob recovered from the shock of his mother's death. Although he continued to hate school, his rebellious attitude changed and he began to care and think about other people. One evening, after school, he noticed a group of people handing out food and clothing to some of the 'down and outs' who slept rough in the streets of Dublin. They were members of a Christian organisation called the Simon Community, who were dedicated to helping homeless people. The next time Bob saw the Simons, he asked them about their work. He approved of the way they never preached or lectured to the people they were helping. Instead, they quietly got on with the job of feeding the homeless and making sure they had enough blankets to keep warm at night.

Bob decided to spend two or three evenings a week helping the Simon Community. Now he had even less time for schoolwork — he did little homework and was often so tired from his late nights that he could not concentrate in class.

4 A Time of Change

In 1969, Bob left school, aged seventeen. It was not a moment too soon, as far as he was concerned. While some of his teachers had approved of his work with the Simons, his refusal to settle down and work hard in class had been a great disappointment to them. Those few teachers who liked Bob were worried about his future.

Their fears seemed to be confirmed when the results of the School Leaving Certificate were announced during the summer holidays. Bob was the only one among his friends to have failed the examination.

Bob's father was too upset to be angry, and Bob himself at last realised how foolish he had been not to have worked harder. Unable to find a permanent job, and not knowing what he wanted to do with his life, he worked part time in a coffee bar and then as a messenger boy for a Dublin photographer.

A year later, still drifting from one dead-end job to another, Bob decided to leave Dublin and try his luck in England. For a few months he worked as a labourer on the building of the M25 motorway. In 1971, he went to London and, unable to afford to rent a flat, moved into a 'squat' (an empty house occupied without the owner's permission). He still did not have a 'proper' job and lived on unemployment benefit or took part time work.

The people who shared the squat with Bob included several who were using drugs, and it was not long before he experimented with them himself. One night, the police raided the house, and Bob and his friends were charged with possession of the drug cannabis. They were found not guilty, but shortly afterwards Bob decided to leave London to make a new start elsewhere.

His sister Lynn was now working as a teacher in Spain, and Bob decided to go and stay with her for a while. Lynn arranged for him to teach English in a language school in Murcia, a city in southern Spain. Bob was surprised to find that he was good at teaching. He also liked Spain and the Spanish people, and stayed in Murcia for several months. Eventually, he became homesick and decided to travel back to Eire.

In Dublin, the only job Bob could find was as a cleaner in an abattoir (a place where animals are slaughtered for meat). He hated working there and felt frustrated at being unable to find anything more enjoyable to do. Once again, he decided to leave Dublin to try to find more interesting work elsewhere. This time he decided to go to Canada.

Bob settled in Vancouver, a city on the west coast of Canada. Although he was unable to obtain a work permit, and so was an illegal immigrant, Bob found work in a bookshop called the Georgia Straight. It was fun, and for the first time in many years he began to feel happy about the life he was leading. He did so well

Bob in Canada

at the bookshop that within a few months he was promoted to manager.

Upstairs from the shop there was a young people's newspaper, also called the Georgia Straight. After Bob had been manager of the bookshop for a while, he was offered a job as a reporter on the newspaper. He wrote articles on pop concerts, reviewed records and interviewed musicians. Again, he did well, and before long was appointed Music Editor, writing most of the articles about pop music for the paper. Bob enjoyed being a journalist so much that he decided he would go back to Dublin and start up a magazine of his own.

5 The Boomtown Rats

When Bob returned to Dublin, he set about starting up his magazine. He realised he would need a good accountant to work out all the finances. Bob had already calculated how many people were likely to buy the magazine each week. An accountant would be able to give him expert advice on how to price the magazine and what capital he would need to start producing it. Bob was confident that after a few months the magazine would attract enough advertising to pay for the office rent and the wages of the staff.

When the accountant had prepared his report, Bob went along to his bank to ask for a loan to start the magazine. He was furious when the bank manager declared that Bob was too young and inexperienced to run a magazine and refused to lend him any money. Bob approached many other people to try to borrow money, even a minister in the Irish government, but they all gave the same response.

While Bob had been trying to start the magazine, he and some friends had formed a rock band. They met once or twice a week to practise and Bob was the lead singer and manager. No one in the group actually expected to make any money. It was just something they did for fun. A big influence on the group was the London band Doctor Feelgood, who played modern versions of black American rhythm and blues songs of the 1940s and 1950s.

Towards the end of 1975, after the band had been practising together for about six months, Bob decided they were ready to play their first gig. He persuaded a further education college in Dublin to book them for their Hallowe'en dance. Up until this time, the group had not bothered to find a name for themselves. Now, a name had to be found, so that the college could put it on their posters advertising the dance. After a lot of discussion, the group decided on Nightlife Thugs, which seemed to describe their rough and raucous rhythm and blues style.

At the dance, the Thugs were amazed by the audience's response to their performance. They cheered loudly and demanded several encores. For the first time, Bob and his friends realised that they might be able to become a professional band — to make records and even to become famous. They decided to try.

Now the group were serious about what they were doing, they decided they needed a better name. Bob suggested the Boomtown Rats, which still had a raw rhythm and blues feel to it but sounded more sophisticated than Nightlife Thugs.

As well as developing into a powerful and original singer, Bob was also becoming an effective manager. He had a flair for thinking of good publicity gimmicks that got the Rats noticed. At some of their gigs, for instance, the Rats showed a promotional film made by

Rentokil (who make rat poison). At others, the group actually let live rats loose to run about under the audience's feet.

These gimmicks certainly provided the band with a lot of publicity, but the Rats were also winning a growing and loyal audience for their music. By now the group was no longer simply copying records made by Doctor Feelgood or American rhythm and blues artists. They were performing songs they had written themselves. Bob was the main songwriter, and he had a talent for composing catchy tunes and memorable, often funny, lyrics.

By the summer of 1976, the Rats had become the top new band in Eire. The local papers were calling them Ireland's answer to the Sex Pistols (the leading band in the punk rock explosion which had hit the music scene in Britain). It was time, Bob decided, to go to London in pursuit of a recording contract with one of the big record companies. Scraping together a few hundred pounds, the Rats went into a Dublin recording studio to make a demonstration tape. Bob would then be able to take it to London to play to the talent scouts at these companies.

He knew that the Rats were a great band, but he found it difficult to convince the London record companies. The first labels he went to — Island and United Artists — turned him down. Bob was on the verge of giving up when Virgin Records offered to sign the group with an advance payment of a million pounds! Another smaller record company, Ensign, also said they wanted to sign the Rats.

The Sex Pistols, the controversial punk rock band which hit the British music scene in 1976

Although the Virgin Records contract would pay the band a lot of money straight away, Bob worked out that the Ensign offer could be much more profitable. Ensign would not pay such a big advance, but they were prepared to give the group a larger share in the profits from their record sales. If the Rats were successful, they would earn considerably more money with this company. Bob liked the people at Ensign: they seemed genuinely to appreciate the Rats' music rather than just wanting to make money out of it. After careful consideration, the Rats decided to sign with Ensign. It was now time to make their first record.

6 'Lookin' After Number One'

Early in 1977, the Boomtown Rats signed a contract with Ensign and the band moved from Dublin to share a house together in Chessington, near London. They wanted to live close to the capital because it is the centre of the British music business. The house contained a good recording studio and it was there the Rats recorded their first album called 'Boomtown Rats'.

Bob's recording experience was limited to the Rats' demonstration tape, which had taken only two or three hours to make. He and the other members of the band were quite unprepared for the amount of work that is involved in making an album. The Rats spent their first two months in England working in the studio six days a week, usually for fifteen hours a day. It was an exhausting experience.

The hard work paid off, however, when the Rats' first single was released. Entitled 'Lookin' After Number One' it went straight into the charts at number 78, and had risen a few weeks later to number 11. Bob and the others could hardly believe their luck. Their very first record was a big hit! The Rats were even asked to appear on the B.B.C. programme 'Top of the Pops'. Their second single, 'Mary Of The Fourth Form', was

The Boomtown Rats

also a hit, reaching number 14.

The Rats achieved popularity so quickly because their music differed from the successful punk bands of the time like the Clash. The Rats' music was close enough to punk to be fashionable, but they recorded songs that had more attractive melodies. At the time, many radio disc jockeys felt that punk records lacked good tunes, but they were enthusiastic about the Rats' records and played them a lot.

With the first two singles behind them, Bob and the Rats went back to Dublin to celebrate with their old friends. They played a concert in the city which was enthusiastically received by their delighted fans. It was during this visit that Bob was introduced to Paula Yates, who was later to become the mother of their daughter Fifi and his wife. But at this time, although Bob liked Paula very much, he did not want to settle down.

The following year was even better for Bob. The Rats' second album, 'Tonic for the Troops', was awarded a gold disc and their next three singles climbed progressively higher in the charts. 'She's So Modern' went to number 12, 'Like Clockwork' to number 6, and with 'Rat Trap' the Rats had their first number 1.

Bob and Paula continued seeing each other and, after the success of 'Tonic for the Troops', they went on holiday together in the West Indies. By now the two were very much in love.

Towards the end of 1978, the Rats spent six weeks in the U.S.A. on a promotional tour to introduce them to the American media, and in particular to American radio disc jockeys. It was very hard work, with the band constantly travelling from one city to another, giving hundreds of radio interviews. But despite their efforts, they were unable to make much of an impression. For some reason, American disc jockeys did not like the Rats as much as their British counterparts and so rarely played the band's records. In America, even more than in Britain where there is a strong pop press, it is essential for a record to get plenty of airplay if it is to be a hit. As a result, the Rats' records sold poorly in the U.S.A.

Back in Britain, the group was going from strength to strength. 1979 was another hugely successful year. 'I Don't Like Mondays' was their second number 1 hit, and was also extremely successful in other countries around the world. The Rats had made a very clever video about the song and this helped to make it a hit in countries they had never toured.

Meanwhile, Bob and Paula had decided to set up house in Clapham, south London. They were very happy together, but being part of the Boomtown Rats meant that Bob had to be away from home a lot, often for long periods of time. Following the success of 'I Don't Like Mondays' the group made a number of lengthy overseas tours — including visits to Sweden, Switzerland, West Germany, France, Australia, New Zealand and Japan. It was as if every country in the world liked the Rats, except the U.S.A.

The year ended with more British hits — 'Diamond Smile' and 'Someone's Lookin' At You' — but despite this, the Boomtown Rats' time as superstars was about to draw to a close.

7 A New Generation

The years 1977 to 1980 had been very exciting and successful for Bob, as the Rats became increasingly popular in Britain, Europe and the Far East. Nearly every record the group had released had been a big hit. It was only in the U.S.A. that they had failed to reach the top of the charts.

However, fashions in pop music change quickly, and it is most unusual for any band to stay at the top for more than two or three years. A new generation of pop fans had grown up and started to buy records. They chose different pop idols and the new star groups like Adam and the Ants, Duran Duran and the Human League were more sophisticated than the Rats.

Bob was aware that popular tastes were changing. In an attempt to keep the Rats at the top he decided that the band should move from Ensign to a bigger record company. They needed to be with a company that had offices all over the world and could afford to spend large amounts of money promoting the group's records. In 1980, the Rats signed a contract with Phonogram but sadly the group continued to sell fewer copies with each new release.

In 1981, the Rats made another trip to the U.S.A.,

and played a lengthy tour of all the major cities. They were well received wherever they performed, but as American disc jockeys still did not play the Rats' records often, they remained unable to get into the charts.

Shortly after he returned from the American tour, Bob was offered a part as a pop singer in a film based on the Pink Floyd album 'The Wall'. Bob was grateful for this extra source of income as the sales of the Rats' fourth album 'Mondo Bongo' had been very disappointing.

Another enjoyable experience was a Rats' tour of the Far East and Australasia. While the group's popularity was falling in Britain, their records continued to be big hits in places like Thailand, Australia and New Zealand. The tour did much to revive the group's flagging spirits.

The Rats' fifth album 'Five Deep' sold even more badly in Britain than 'Mondo Bongo', and for the first time one of the Rats' singles, 'Never In A Million Years', was a complete flop. The next single, 'House On Fire', did a little better, but it was obvious now that the Rats' days at the top were over.

1982 was a thoroughly miserable year for Bob as he saw the Rats steadily falling in popularity. The only good thing that happened was the birth of his daughter Fifi. Fortunately, Paula's career was developing successfully. She had become a presenter on the progressive television pop show 'The Tube'. Once Fifi was born, Bob and Paula decided it was time to move out of London and live in the country. They felt it would be a

Bob, Paula and Fifi

better place for a child to grow up. Although Bob was heavily in debt to Phonogram, he managed to scrape together enough money to buy a house in Faversham, Kent.

The following two years seemed to confirm the group's fears that their career was over. Every single the band released was a flop. But while Bob worried about his future in the music business, something was happening that would make his own troubles seem petty and unimportant. It would also dramatically change his whole life.

8 'Do They Know It's Christmas?'

The chain of events which led to Bob's involvement with Band Aid and Live Aid had started one evening towards the end of 1984. Bob and Paula were watching television at home when the B.B.C. showed a film by reporter Michael Buerk about the famine that was devastating Ethiopia. Buerk described the terrible extent of the famine, which was clearly portrayed by dreadful pictures of emaciated, dying children.

Up until that night, very few people outside Africa knew about this famine. Established relief agencies like the Save the Children Fund were doing what they could to help, but the size of the disaster was too enormous for them to cope alone. Governments in rich countries like Britain and America seemed to be ignoring the tragedy. Buerk's film made it clear that this was the worst famine Africa had ever experienced during recorded history. Unless a massive international relief operation was started immediately, millions of men, women and children would continue to starve to death.

Along with many other people who watched Buerk's report, Bob and Paula were deeply moved by the horror of what they saw. When the film was over, Paula burst into tears. For his part, Bob felt very angry and ashamed. He was disgusted that not one government in the world outside Africa seemed to be doing anything to help.

That night Bob was unable to sleep, haunted by the pictures of death and suffering that he had seen. When he went downstairs in the morning, Paula had already left to go to work, but in the kitchen she had pinned up a notice which read: 'Everyone who visits this house from today onwards will be asked to give £5 until we have raised £200 for famine relief.'

Later that day at Phonogram, Bob talked to other people who had watched the television report the night before. Everyone was appalled by what they had seen.

Casually, without really considering what he was saying, Bob remarked, 'I'm thinking about making a record to raise money to help.'

'Yes, you should,' came the reply.

At first, Bob had only the vaguest idea of what sort of record to release. He realised that, on their own, the Rats could do little to help. They were no longer a chart-topping band, so who would take any notice of what they said or did? He decided that he must ask other stars to sing on the record with them.

Bob phoned up singers and musicians that he knew, asking for their help. He was far from sure that any of them would agree, because pop stars are constantly being asked to perform for free. The first person he approached was Midge Ure of Ultravox. Midge immediately said he would help, and also offered to co-write the record with Bob. Duran Duran, Boy George,

Sting and Spandau Ballet were the next people Bob contacted, and they agreed to appear on the record. All of them had seen or heard of the television report about the famine and all had been shocked by it.

Bob asked Phonogram if they would be willing to be involved. He knew he would need the full co-operation of the label if the record was to be released quickly. He

Bob with Midge Ure

wanted to get it into the shops for Christmas, when most money could be raised. There was no time to lose — every day spent making the record was another day in which thousands of people would die.

The next two weeks were the busiest Bob had ever experienced. The group was to be called Band Aid, and Bob and Midge were already working on the song. Meanwhile, Bob was also having to make hundreds of phone calls and attend endless meetings. Each night, he could only snatch three or four hours of sleep. Two things kept him going during this fortnight — the thought of people starving in Africa, and the wonderfully generous response of everybody he asked to help with Band Aid. Everyone agreed to donate their time and services freely, including the singers and musicians who would make the record and the shops which would sell it. Even the factory that was going to press the disc agreed to do it for free, while the I.C.I. company donated the vinyl. Only the Government refused to help, insisting that V.A.T. (Value Added Tax) must be paid on every copy that was sold.

'Do They Know It's Christmas?' was actually recorded less than three weeks after Bob first learnt about the famine — a remarkably short time considering all the organisation that was involved. The recording session was on 25 November and, in order to get the record into the shops as quickly as possible, it had to be completed that day.

Bob was the first person to arrive at the recording studio. For a few minutes he was worried that no one would actually turn up, but he soon relaxed. Everybody

The Band Aid recording session included such famous names as Sting and Bananarama

who had agreed to help arrived on time, except Boy George. He had overslept and had to be woken by a phone call from Bob! Soon the studio was packed with the biggest names in the British pop business including George Michael, Paul Young, U2, Spandau Ballet, and Paul Weller. The session started in the morning and by the early hours of the next day the recording of 'Do They Know It's Christmas?' was being rushed to the pressing plant for production.

The publicity that Bob had arranged to accompany the release of the record was immense. Almost every newspaper in the country printed reports and pictures of the recording session, and the *Daily Mirror* devoted the whole of their front page to it. Television and radio coverage was widespread, and BBC 1 showed the Band Aid video just before that week's edition of 'Top of the Pops'. By the time the record was in the shops, everybody in Britain knew about it.

The public response was remarkable. Grocery, chemist and butchers' shops displayed the record sleeves all over their windows. Some people bought boxes of 50 copies and gave the records away to their friends as Christmas presents. Jim Diamond, who was at number 1 in the charts with 'I Should Have Known Better', told the press, 'I don't want people to buy my record next week, I want them to buy the Band Aid one instead.'

As Bob had hoped, the record went straight to number 1, and as the days went by the demand kept growing. At one point, the pressing plant was producing 300,000 copies a day, and still that was not enough.

Reaction in America was also tremendous. A million and a half copies were sold there within two weeks of release. Six million copies were sold worldwide.

By January 1985, 'Do They Know It's Christmas?' had raised over 5 million pounds for Band Aid — five times more than Bob had originally hoped for. He now had to decide how best to spend all this money. He had pledged that every penny would be spent on famine relief and he wanted to keep that promise. Bob decided to visit the famine areas himself, to see what kind of help was most urgently needed.

9 Live Aid

On Christmas Eve 1984 Bob arrived by plane in Addis Ababa, the capital of Ethiopia. One of the first people he met there was Mother Teresa, a nun who is famous throughout the world for her work with poor people in the slums of Calcutta in India. Now, Mother Teresa was directing a relief operation in Ethiopia.

Bob visited two refugee camps, at Lalibela and Mekele. He was absolutely horrified by the suffering that he saw. Thousands of people were lying around on the bare earth close to death. Most of them had no food to eat, no blankets to keep them warm, and no medicine to treat their illnesses. They were pathetically thin, and covered in boils and sores which their starved bodies had no ability to heal. They were so weak that they did not even have the energy to brush away the flies which clustered round their eyes, noses and mouths.

Worst of all were the people's eyes. They were expressionless, with not a flicker of hope or life in them. They just stared out blankly at the surrounding horror. Looking at these helpless people, Bob found tears were streaming down his face.

The doctors and nurses who were trying to help explained to him how hopeless their task was. They

A young famine victim

only had enough food and medicine for a tiny proportion of the people in the camps, and had to make the terrible choice of who to give food and medicine to, knowing that those they rejected would certainly die. And thousands of starving people were continuing to arrive at the camps every day.

Having learnt all he could, and been told what sorts of food and medicine were most desperately needed, Bob flew back to London to start the Band Aid operation without delay. He realised how little he knew about famine relief, so he set up a Board of Trustees, which consisted of experts on nutrition (diet), medicine and transport. Transport was crucial to the success of Band Aid, for there was little point in sending food and medicine to Africa if, once there, they could not be distributed quickly and efficiently.

Meanwhile, in the U.S.A., a group of pop stars had organised their own version of Band Aid, called U.S.A. for Africa. Michael Jackson and Lionel Ritchie had written a song for the group to record, called 'We Are The World', and Bob was invited to the recording session. The record featured the biggest American stars, including Michael Jackson, Diana Ross, Bob Dylan, Stevie Wonder, Tina Turner, Bruce Springsteen and Paul Simon.

Having seen the horror of the Ethiopian refugee camps, Bob knew that it was not enough for Band Aid to simply release a record. A lot more had to be done if the 22 million people starving to death in Africa were going to be saved. Why not, thought Bob, organise an all-star concert featuring the world's most famous singers and musicians? The concert could be broadcast live on television and the viewers would be asked to donate money to the Band Aid fund. A really big concert like this would raise a lot more money than the records 'Do They Know It's Christmas?' and 'We Are The World'.

Bob knew that organising Live Aid would be far more complicated than the Band Aid recording session. A stadium would have to be found, pop stars would have to be contacted, sound equipment set up, tickets and t-shirts printed, television and radio coverage arranged — the list was endless. Bob then decided that to achieve maximum impact, and to raise as much money as possible, Live Aid should consist of two concerts happening simultaneously in Britain and the U.S.A.!

Luckily, Harvey Goldsmith, the most experienced concert promoter in Britain, heard that Bob was planning Live Aid and offered to help. Harvey took on the responsibility of organising the concert so Bob was free to concentrate on creating publicity for the event. In London and New York, Bob spent much of his time talking to the major television and radio stations, offering them the rights to broadcast Live Aid in return for donations to the Band Aid fund. Eventually, he was able to secure over seventeen hours of live coverage on BBC 1 and Radio 1 in Britain, and similar coverage in the U.S.A. and many other countries. Bob insisted that all the broadcasts should include frequent requests for the audience to donate money to Band Aid, and information about where the money should be sent.

The actual numbers of people who watched Live Aid on 13 July 1985 exceeded even Bob's wildest hopes. It has been estimated that 2 billion people tuned in, and that 85% of the world's television sets were switched on to Live Aid at some point during the concert.

By the end of the day, the British Live Aid concert had raised 4 million pounds for Band Aid. Within a week, that figure had risen to 30 million pounds. It was reported that people who could not afford to give

Bob with David Bowie and Alison Moyet at the Live Aid concert

This map marks some of the African countries which Bob Geldof has visited on behalf of Band Aid

money gave away their gold wedding rings to be melted down. Old people gave money from their pensions. At least one couple sold their house and gave the proceeds to Band Aid.

Now, much more than just a gesture of sympathy to Africa's starving, Band Aid was in a position to save the lives of millions of people who would otherwise die of starvation and disease.

10 'This is the World Calling'

Bob's work for famine relief did not finish after the Live Aid concert. It was at least a year before he was able to stop working full time for Band Aid and devote more time to his family and his own career. Meanwhile, he had to make sure that all the money that was given to Band Aid was being spent in the most effective way.

With the other members of the Band Aid Board of Trustees, Bob decided to direct the relief operation in two ways. Firstly, food and medicine would be sent to Africa to save people who were still starving. Secondly, money would be sent to pay for schemes to provide better harvests in the famine areas for future years. Bob had to spend much of his time abroad, particularly in Africa, making sure that the relief was reaching the right people. He visited Mali, Burkina Faso, Niger, Chad, Sudan and Ethiopia, finding out what help was needed and then organising it as quickly as possible.

Bob was also asked to help with other famine relief campaigns which were inspired by and modelled on Band Aid — like Sport Aid and School Aid. He was closely involved with the Sport Aid campaign for Africa in 1986 when people ran at organised fun runs all over the world to raise money. Bob knew that if the media

Thousands of runners took part in the Sport Aid campaign for Africa in 1986

and public associated him with these other campaigns, it would be easier for them to be taken seriously and get widespread publicity.

Bob spent a lot of time meeting representatives from governments of the richer countries in the world. He tried to persuade them to spend more time and money ensuring that famines do not happen again. He told these governments that if they organised the right sort of farming schemes now, famine would be a thing of the past. The U.S.A., as the richest country in the world, was the most important overseas power that he visited. Bob made several lengthy trips to Washington, talking to senators and congressmen. He went to Australia, where he met the Prime Minister, Bob Hawke, as well as visiting a number of European countries.

It was difficult for government ministers to refuse his requests because so many people around the world

Bob with Margaret Thatcher

supported Bob and Band Aid. He was able to make these governments give far more money and attention to famine relief and crop growing schemes than they may otherwise have done.

Bob also tried to persuade the British government to donate the V.A.T. from the sales of 'Do They Know It's Christmas?' to famine relief. At first, the Conservative government refused, saying that if they did this for Band Aid then every charity in Britain would want the same treatment. Eventually, support for Bob among the British people grew so strong that the government was forced to change its mind.

Many people were surprised when Bob was not awarded any sort of decoration in the Christmas Honours List in 1985. It was said that Margaret Thatcher had refused to decorate him because of the embarrassment he had caused her government over the V.A.T. issue. Whether this is true or not, the public outcry over the matter was immense. A year later, in The Queen's Birthday Honours List, Bob was awarded a K.B.E. (Knight Commander of the British Empire).

Another honour Bob received came from the Congressional Black Caucus in Washington, a body representing black Congressmen in the House of Representatives. Bob was the first white man ever to be honoured by the Caucus. He was also nominated for the Nobel Peace Prize in 1985, 1986 and 1987. Although he was not actually awarded the Prize, it was a tremendous honour that someone so young had been seriously considered for it.

When Bob started to receive these awards he was

Bob receives his K.B.E. at Buckingham Palace

unsure about whether to accept them. He knew that hundreds of people had worked very hard for Band Aid, and it seemed unfair that they were not being awarded honours as well. In the end, he decided that he would accept them on behalf of Band Aid rather than for himself personally.

Gradually, Bob found he was able to spend more time with Paula and Fifi, and to concentrate on his own musical career again. He also found time to write his autobiography called 'Is That It?' in which he gave an honest and humorous account of his life. The book was published in 1986 and it very quickly became a bestseller. In the same year, he and Paula were married in Las Vegas.

Sadly, Bob had grown apart from the other members of the Boomtown Rats during the past few years. When he returned to the music business, it was as a solo artist, not as the leader of the Rats. In November 1986 he released his solo album 'Deep In The Heart Of Nowhere', which featured contributions from friends like Eric Clapton, Alison Moyet, Midge Ure, the Eurythmics, Brian Setzer (of the Stray Cats) and Jools Holland. Bob also released two tracks from the album as singles — 'This Is The World Calling' and 'Love Like A Rocket'.

'Deep In The Heart Of Nowhere' was awarded a gold disc in Britain and a silver disc in Norway, and 'This Is The World Calling', 'The Beat of the Night' and 'Love Like A Rocket' were big hits in Italy. His records continued to sell steadily in 1986 and 1987, particularly in America where they sold in excess of 260,000 copies.

He also had four top ten hits in Europe.

Meanwhile, Bob continues to spend time working for Band Aid. Each month he attends the meeting of the Board of Trustees, planning relief and development schemes as well as monitoring the success of those already in operation.

To many Bob Geldof will always be the pop star who captured the public imagination. It was his inspiration which led to one of the most remarkable fund-raising events of all time, while his tireless dedication helped to remind us all that we are one world, one people. With great determination he showed that we all have a part to play in the great campaign to rid the world from famine. This extraordinary achievement will never be forgotten.

Important events in the life of Bob Geldof

1952	Born on 5 October in Dublin
1975	Forms the band the Boomtown Rats
1977	Boomtown Rats sign a recording contract with Ensign
1978	The Rats' second album 'Tonic For The Troops' is awarded a gold disc. Their single 'Rat Trap' becomes their first number 1.
1979	The Rats' second number 1 single is 'I Don't Like Mondays'. Bob sets up house with Paula Yates in Clapham, south London.
1980	Boomtown Rats leave Ensign and sign a recording contract with Phonogram
1981	Bob plays the leading role in the film 'The Wall', based on the Pink Floyd album
1982	Fifi, Bob and Paula's daughter, is born
1984	The Michael Buerk report on the famine in Ethiopia is broadcast on B.B.C. television. Bob forms Band Aid to record the single 'Do They Know It's Christmas?' to raise money for famine victims. Visits Ethiopia to find out what relief is most urgently needed.

1985	The rock concert, Live Aid, is held in London and Philadelphia on 13 July. It raises over 50 million pounds for famine relief.
1986	Bob helps to promote the Sport Aid campaign for Africa.
	Awarded K.B.E. in The Queen's Birthday Honours List.
	Publishes his autobiography 'Is That It?'
	Bob and Paula marry
	Releases his solo album 'Deep In The Heart Of Nowhere'
1985-7	Nominated for the Nobel Peace Prize.

Summary of Band Aid's Aims

Since its formation as a charity in 1984, Band Aid has led the way in fund-raising activities to help famine-hit countries. It aims to help people in six African countries: Ethiopia, Sudan, Mali, Burkina Faso, Chad and Niger.

Every year it receives hundreds of requests for money, so the Board of Trustees has to be very careful about what it decides is a worthwhile cause. It is currently transferring some of the decision-making on the choice of projects to local Band Aid groups in Africa.

Approximately 75 million pounds sterling were raised worldwide over the past four years, and about two thirds of this has been spent on emergency assistance, eg food, shelter equipment, vehicles, medical equipment, and transport costs. The remaining third is being spent on longer-term 'development' projects.

These projects are concerned with supporting farming, improving health care, and encouraging training in useful skills. Band Aid aims particularly to support local people's own attempts at helping themselves. The charity is also keen to encourage research aimed at solving particular problems in these areas, and to help increase communication between local communities so that each can learn from the other's experience.

Band Aid follows the progress of all the projects it has funded, and will be preparing a review of its work when all the donations have finally been spent (by December 1988).

If you would like further information about Band Aid please write with a stamped addressed envelope to:-

Band Aid
PO Box 4TX
LONDON W1A 4TX